X

A New True Book

PLANTS WITHOUT SEEDS

By Helen J. Challand

CHILDRENS PRESS ®

CHICAGO

Mosses, mushrooms, and ferns
are plants without seeds.

Library of Congress Cataloging-in-Publication Data

Challand, Helen J.
  Plants without seeds.

  (A New true book)
  Includes index.
  Summary: Examines the characteristics of simple plants
that do not have seeds, including algae, fungi, lichen,
mosses, and ferns, with a brief look at bacteria.
  1. Cryptogams—Juvenile literature. 2. Bacteria—
Juvenile literature. [1. Cryptogams. 2. Plants]
I. Title.
QK505.5.C48 1986   586   85-30935
ISBN 0-516-01286-X   AACR2

PHOTO CREDITS
Valan Photos:
© Albert Kuhnigk—2, 42 (left)
© Herman H. Giethoorn—4 (bottom), 40 (left)
© Harold V. Green—7, 9, 12, 38 (right), 45 (left)
© J.A. Wilkinson—16 (left), 29 (left)
© Alan Wilkinson—16 (right)
© J.R. Page—28 (left)
© Tom W. Parkin—36 (left)
© Francois Morneau—42 (right)
© Professor R.C. Simpson—Cover, 45 (right)
EKM-Nepenthe:
© Robert Eckert—4 (top)
© W. South—6 (right)
© R. L. Potts—38 (left)
Tom Stack & Associates:
© Tom Stack—6 (left), 15, 19 (left), 35 (right)
© William Patterson—13
© Brian Parker—19 (right), 43
© Don & Pat Valenti—29 (right)
© Evelyn Tronca—32 (right)
Journalism Services:
© Harry J. Przekop—10
Photri—11, 31, 32 (left)
© Jerry Hennen—21, 28 (right)
Root Resources:
© John Kuhout—23, 25
© Louise K. Broman—26 (left)
© Jerome Wyckoff—26 (right), 39
© Bob & Ira Spring—35 (left)
© Lynn Stone—36 (right)

TABLE OF CONTENTS

Unlike the green plants that surround them, these fungi do not have true roots, stems, or leaves. They do not have chlorophyll, the green coloring that allows plants with seeds to make their own food. Fungi get food from the green plants.

PLANTS ARE LIVING THINGS

Plants are living things. Most plants have a green coloring called chlorophyll. This helps plants make their own food. Plants can turn water and carbon dioxide from the air into sugar with the help of light and chlorophyll. Animals cannot do this. They depend on plants.

All plants may be divided into two groups: plants that have seeds and plants without seeds. This book will tell you about many of the simple plants that do not have seeds.

Neither lichens (left) nor red moss (right) have seeds.

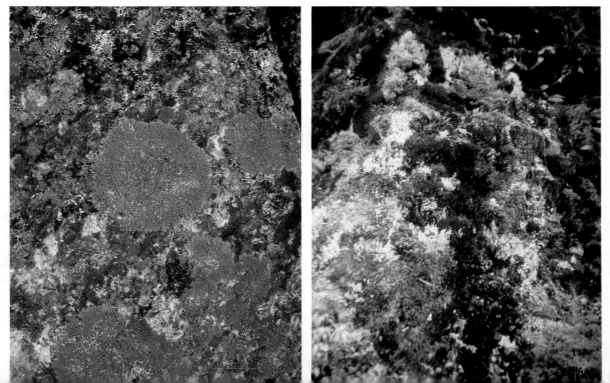

This green
algae
floats on the
surface of a
freshwater
swamp.

ALGAE

Algae are the simplest
and oldest plants. Many
are so small one needs a
microscope to see them.
Others can grow over one
hundred feet long. Algae
may live as a single cell,
in groups or colonies, in
sheets or long strands.

Algae do not have true roots, stems, or leaves. They do not have any flowers, fruits, or seeds.

Algae reproduce in a number of ways. A large cell may split into two cells. This is called fission. A cell may divide over and over again making a whole group of cells. This is called sporing. In some cases one cell will join another cell and then divide. This is called conjugation.

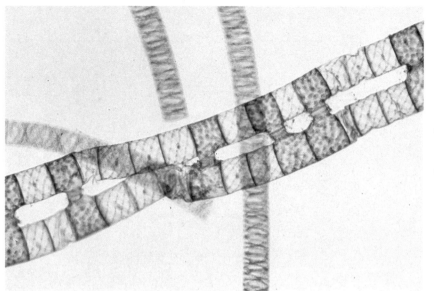

A green alga,
magnified 80 times,
reproducing by
conjugation

Algae grow in freshwater
or in saltwater. They grow
on the bark of trees, in the
soil, or on top of snow. Algae
can live in hot springs, caves,
and mines. There are over
thirty thousand kinds of
algae. Algae are divided
into groups by their color.

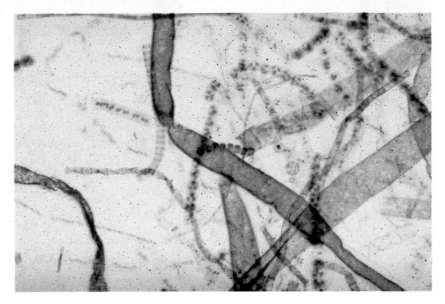

Magnified view of blue-green algae

Blue-green algae

Blue-green algae is the oldest. Two that you can find in pond water are nostoc and oscillatoria. Some blue-green algae can live in water that reaches 163 degrees

Small pond covered with algae.

Fahrenheit. Others can live in polluted waters. This helps us figure out how dirty the water is getting.

Green algae

Green algae is the group that higher plants probably came from. Spirogyra is a

Spirogyra, a green algae, magnified 80 times.

long filament with a
ribbon-shaped chloroplastid.
It can be found in streams,
ponds, and marshes.
Protococcus is a one-
celled alga that grows on
the north side of some trees.
Some green algae live
inside hydras, sponges,
snails, and flatworms. They

get along fine together. The algae make the food for the animal. The animal provides water and nitrogen for the algae.

Yellow-green and golden-brown algae

These algae are grouped together. Diatoms are in this group. They are often

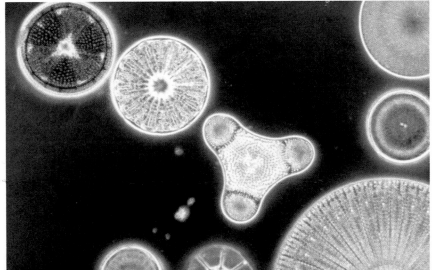

Close-up of diatoms

called "jewels" of the sea. The hard cell wall is made of silicon, a material found in glass.

Euglena

The euglena is often put in a group by itself. It is an odd little creature. Is it a plant or animal? At one end it has a long whip called a flagellum. This helps the euglena move around as an animal. When it is in the dark it can take in food and eat

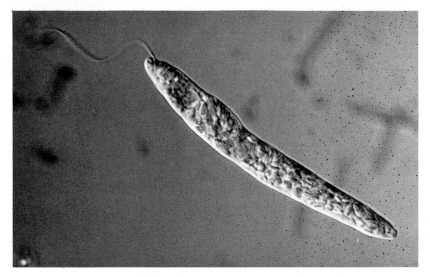

Euglena, magnified 600 times. Its whip, or flagellum, is at the top left.

as an animal. Euglenas have chlorophyll and can make sugar the same as other green plants. They may be the link between animals and plants.

Red algae

Many red algae live in the warm parts of the

ocean. They are much larger. Some look like little bushes. Some can live three hundred feet down where there is very little light. Still they are able to get enough light to make their own food. The red pigment hides the green coloring or chlorophyll.

Red seaweed (left) and rockweed (right)

Brown algae

These algae are big. They grow in colder ocean waters. Rockweed attaches itself to rocks along a shoreline. Kelp grow one hundred feet or longer. Attached to the bottom of the ocean, the big kelp plant floats to the surface by means of air bladders. The Sargasso Sea is filled with brown algae. It covers two million square miles.

WHAT GOOD ARE ALGAE?

Fish eat algae. These plants are the first link in the food chain.

Humans get a material from algae called algin. It gives the smooth taste or feel to ice cream, puddings, face creams, and shoe polish.

Many algae, such as sea lettuce, are used to make

Sea lettuce is used to
make food for humans.

cookies, cakes, crackers,
and other foods.

Algae produce much of
the oxygen we need for
breathing. While they are
making their food they
give off oxygen.

Algae are high in
nitrogen and potassium.

People collect and dry the algae and sell it as fertilizer.

The silicon found in the cell walls of diatoms is used to make explosives, insulation, soundproofing, polishing powder, and paints.

It is now believed that the oil and gas formed millions of years ago in the ground were created by algae.

Winter mushrooms growing on a rotting log

FUNGI

Have you ever seen mold growing on bread, a toadstool coming out of a rotten log, or the yeast a baker puts in bread dough? These are all plants called fungi.

21

Fungi do not have true roots, stems, or leaves. Neither do they have flowers, fruits, or seeds. None of them has chlorophyll, that green color that helps plants make food. Fungi must get their food in one of two ways. A fungus that eats dead plants or animals is called a saprophyte. One that eats off living things, such as ringworm or

Bread mold

athlete's foot, is called a parasite.

Algae-like fungi

These plants can live on land or in water. They have spores that move around with the help of one or two flagella. Bread mold is an algae-like fungus. Water mold attacks fish, eating away their fins and other body parts. Downy mildew lives on and harms grapes, lettuce, onions, and cucumbers. The potato blight destroys food crops.

Sac fungi

These plants may be single celled or many celled. Some sac fungi are helpful, others are harmful. Penicillium is a mold that grows well on citrus

Green mold on a lemon

fruits. As it eats it gives off a liquid that has been named penicillin. It is used as an antibiotic when people are sick. The Dutch elm fungus attacks and kills elm trees.

A morel looks like a mushroom. Some morels

Morel (left) and the poisonous
destroying angel (above)

are good to eat. Truffles
are other fungi that can be
eaten. They grow under the
ground. In France pigs and
dogs are trained to sniff
out a patch of them.

Yeast works on sugar. It
gives off carbon dioxide
and alcohol. In baking

bread the carbon dioxide gets trapped in the dough and causes it to rise. The alcohol evaporates during the baking.

Club fungi

Mushrooms, toadstools, and tree brachets are club fungi. Only certain kinds of mushrooms are safe to eat. One type, an amanita, is called the destroying angel. A single plant has enough poison to kill a person.

Young puffballs can be eaten. The one at left is releasing its spores. This is how it reproduces.

Puffballs look like the tops of giant mushrooms, without the stalks. Some grow three feet across. Young, tender puffballs can be eaten.

Smut is a black blob that grows on corn, eating away the kernels and young cob. Rust is a destructive plant that lives off two different plants. It starts on wheat, then must find a barberry bush to finish its life cycle.

Rust (left) and corn smut (right)

Imperfect fungi

Most of the plants in this group are not very pleasant to humans. Ringworm is a fungus that can cause sore spots on the heads of children. When it grows between toes it is called athlete's foot. It can cause the skin to crack and bleed. Another imperfect fungus is called barber's itch, for it eats on the face around the whiskers.

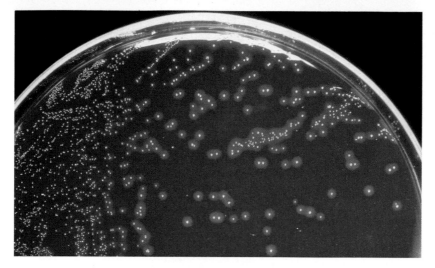

Bacteria growing in blood sample. Bacteria usually reproduce by dividing into two parts.

Bacteria are among the smallest of living things. Their shape may be round, rodlike, or spiral. Bacteria live in the soil, water, or air from the North to the South Poles. Most cannot make their own food. They

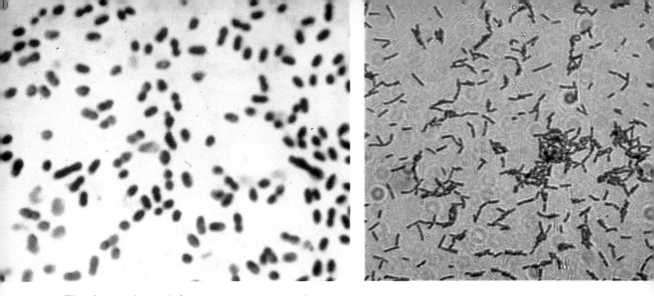

The bacteria at left causes pneumonia.
The bacteria on the right can be used to make cheese.

eat off living or dead things. A few use material that has never been alive.

Bacteria cause diseases such as strep throat, whooping cough, typhoid fever, and salmonella or food poisoning. There are, however, many good or helpful bacteria. Just think how many dead things would pile up on the earth if bacteria didn't break them down. This decay returns the dead material back to the soil. Bacteria that make lactic acid will cause milk to sour so cheeses can be made. Our large intestine has helpful bacteria in it to keep us healthy. There are probably more good bacteria than bad ones, if all the different kinds are counted.

LICHENS

When two things live together and each gets something from the other, this is one type of symbiosis. A lichen is made of an alga and a fungus. The alga makes the food for the fungus. The fungus gets water and minerals for the alga. It is a very happy partnership.

Lichens are called the pioneers of the soil. They live on rocks and help

Lichen can grow on snow (left)
or on tree bark (above).

break them up into tiny
bits. Lichens can go for
long periods of time
without water. They live on
soil, trees, stone buildings,
fence posts, and on snow.
Up north lichen is called
reindeer moss and may be

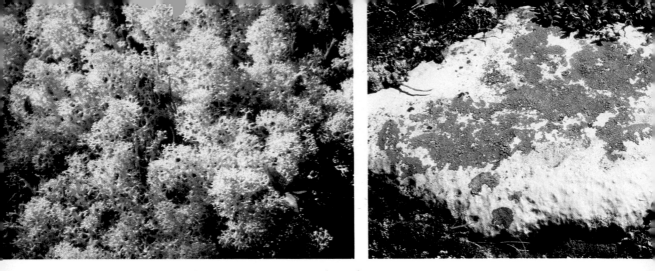

Reindeer moss (left) and other lichens (right)

the only thing around for those animals to eat.

Lichens are used in dyeing animal hides in leather making. They are also used to make litmus paper, the red and blue strips used to test whether a material is an acid or a base.

MOSSES

Mosses are short little plants. They are more complex than algae and fungi. Moss has chlorophyll so it can make its own food. It does not have the tubes or canals found in higher plants. That is why moss never grows large in size.

Moss reproduces in two ways. This is called

Spores on mosses

alternation of generations.
Spores are made in one
generation. Then the
spores produce female and
male plants. They make the
eggs and sperms. These
get together and grow into
the sexless plant, a stalk

Cushion moss covers the rocks on a forest floor.

with a capsule of spores at the top of it. This goes on and on in a circle or cycle.

Moss is helpful. It breaks up rocks, prevents erosion, makes soil richer, and is great at holding water.

Sphagnum moss

Sphagnum moss is found
in bogs. Millions of years
ago it formed coal by heat
and pressure. Granite
moss, found in the alpine
and arctic regions, is eaten
by wildlife.

FERNS

Ferns are the most complex of the simple plants. They have true roots, stems, and leaves. They have conducting tubes for water and food. As with the others they do not have flowers, fruits, or seeds, at least today. However, ferns are very old plants. Four hundred million years ago they were the most important

Tree fern (left) and cinnamon fern (right)

plants on the earth. Ferns
lived with the dinosaurs
and other reptiles during
the Mesozoic era. At that
time ferns were as big as
trees and had seeds.

Close-up of fern spores

Ferns have an interesting cycle of reproduction. The large land fern has spores on the underside of its leaves. These often look like little brown spots. Each spore must fall into water (a puddle will do) in

order to grow into a tiny
fern plant. This plant, the
sexual generation, makes
the eggs and sperms.
When a sperm fertilizes an
egg, it will grow into the
big fern plant.

Ferns helped the mosses
years ago to form coal
beds. They help make soil
and keep it from being
washed away.

All the seedless plants
described in this book lead
the way for those plants

The ostrich fern (right) and a close-up of its fiddlehead (left)

with seeds. Because of
them we can have an
apple tree, rose bush, stalk
of corn, and a marigold
today.

WORDS YOU SHOULD KNOW

algae(AL • jee) — the simplest and oldest plants; grouped by their colors, they do not have roots, stems, leaves, flowers, fruits, or seeds

athlete's foot(ATH • leets FOOT) — a fungus; ringworm that affects the feet

bacteria(bak • TIER • ee • uh) — microscopic plants that live in water, soil, or the bodies of animals and plants; some cause diseases, others are helpful to humans

barber's itch(BAR • bers ICH) — a fungus that causes sores on the face around the whiskers

chlorophyll(KLOR • uh • fill) — the green coloring in plants that helps to make their food

conjugation(kahn • jun • GAY • shun) — a means of algae reproducing by one cell joining another and then dividing

ferns(FURNS) — simple plants with roots, stems, and leaves, but with no seeds, flowers, or fruits; ferns reproduce by spores

filament(FILL • uh • munt) — a long, thin cell that is shaped like a cylinder

fission(FISH • un) — algae reproduction by a large cell splitting into two cells

fungi(FUN • ji) — simple plants, including molds and mushrooms, that have no chlorophyll

lichens(LIE • kens) — plants that consist of an alga and a fungus living together in symbiosis

mosses(MOSS • uz) — small green plants that reproduce via alternation of generations

ringworm(RING • werm) — a fungus that causes sore spots on the head; called athlete's foot when it affects the feet

smut(SMUHT) — a fungus that affects plants with black blobs of spores

sporing(SPORE • ing) — algae reproduction by a cell dividing over and over to make new cells

symbiosis(sim • bigh • OH • sus) — the living together of two unlike things that benefits both

yeast(YEEST) — a fungus used in baking to make dough rise

INDEX

About the Author
Helen J. Challand earned her M.A. and Ph.D. from Northwestern
University. She currently is Chair of the Science Department at
National College of Education and Coordinator of Undergraduate
Studies for the college's West Suburban Campus.
    An experienced classroom teacher and science consultant, Dr.
Challand has worked on science projects for Scott Foresman and
Company, Rand McNally Publishers, Harper-Row Publishers,
Encyclopedia Britannica Films, Coronet Films, and Journal Films.
She is the author of Earthquakes, Plants without Seeds, and
Experiments with Magnets in the True Book series and served as
associate editor for the Young People's Science Encyclopedia
published by Childrens Press.